M000165809

foreword

Ask a little kid what the first letter of the alphabet stands for and the response is immediate: A is for apple—it's as simple as that. What puts this popular fruit at the head of the class is not only its taste, but its versatility. Whether it's appetizers and entrees or fabulous desserts, apples can flavour each course with their lovely sweet essence.

At Company's Coming, we've chosen our favourite apple recipes and compiled them in this handy little book for you to enjoy. As a starter for this weekend's get-together, for instance, try our Brie in Pastry, served with fresh apple slices. Then move on to our easy Apple Pork Chops and finish with a spectacular Caramel Apple Pie, or choose from any of the wonderful recipes featured here. Friends and family will clamour for more, because everyone falls for an apple's appeal.

Jean Paré

brie in pastry

A great make-ahead recipe. Assemble pastry and cheese, wrap well and freeze. On the day of your event, thaw, brush with egg and bake as directed.

Puff pastry patty shells, thawed	2	2
Brie cheese round	4 oz.	125 g
Large egg, fork-beaten	1	1
Medium unpeeled red apples, thinly sliced (see Tip, page 64)	2	2

Roll out 1 pastry shell on lightly floured surface to 5 1/2 to 6 inch (14 to 15 cm) circle.

Place cheese in centre of pastry. Bring up sides, pleating dough around edge. Roll out second pastry shell. Cut circle in pastry to fit top of cheese. Place on top of cheese. Crimp edge to seal. Cut decorative shapes from scraps of pastry. Place on top.

Brush pastry with egg. Place on greased baking sheet. Bake in 450°F (230°C) oven for 15 minutes. Reduce heat to 350°F (175°C). Bake for about 5 minutes until pastry is golden. Transfer to serving plate.

Arrange apple around pastry. Serves 6.

1 serving: 200 Calories; 13.1 g Total Fat (3.4 g Mono, 4 g Poly, 4.8 g Sat); 57 mg Cholesterol; 15 g Carbohydrate; 1 g Fibre; 7 g Protein; 183 mg Sodium

paté and apple tartlets

You can cut these tartlets into quarters for casual finger food, or serve them whole as an appetizer for a sit-down dinner.

Package of puff pastry, thawed according to package directions	14 oz.	397 g
Liver paté (cognac or country-style), softened	6 oz.	170 g
Medium unpeeled tart apples (such as Granny Smith), very thinly sliced	1 1/2	1 1/2
Large egg, fork-beaten	1	1

Roll out 1 square of puff pastry on lightly floured surface to 1/8 inch (3 mm) thickness. Cut into quarters. Slightly trim corners of each quarter to make rough circles. Place on lightly greased baking sheet. Repeat with remaining square of pastry.

Remove and discard any gelatin from paté. Divide paté into 8 pieces. Place 1 piece in centre of each pastry circle. Spread paté to within 1/2 inch (12 mm) of edge.

Arrange apple in fan shape over paté.

Brush apple and pastry with egg. Bake in 400°F (205°C) oven for 15 to 20 minutes until pastry is golden. Makes 8 tartlets.

1 tartlet: 371 Calories; 25.8 g Total Fat (7.3 g Mono, 11.7 g Poly, 5.0 g Sat); 83 mg Cholesterol; 28 g Carbohydrate; 1 g Fibre; 8 g Protein; 284 mg Sodium

apple-spiced tea

Rich amber colour with a distinct apple aroma—just the thing for chilly afternoons!

Apple juice	4 1/2 cups	1.1 L
Cinnamon stick (4 inches, 10 cm), broken up	1	1
Granulated sugar	1 tsp.	5 mL
Orange pekoe tea bags	2	2

Combine first 3 ingredients in medium saucepan. Bring to a boil. Remove from heat.

Add tea bags. Let steep for 10 minutes. Remove and discard tea bags. Strain liquid through sieve into heavy glasses. Discard solids. Makes about 4 1/2 cups (1.1 L).

1 cup (250 mL): *120 Calories; 0.3 g Total Fat (trace Mono, 0.1 g Poly, 0.1 g Sat); 0 mg Cholesterol; 30 g Carbohydrate; trace Fibre; trace Protein; 7 mg Sodium*

apple and shrimp salad with creamy dill dressing

Great as a lunch, light supper, or first course before grilled fish, pork tenderloin or chicken. For extra crunch, add some chopped celery or sliced water chestnuts.

Cut or torn romaine lettuce, lightly packed	15 cups	3.74 L
Cooked large shrimps, peeled and deveined	1 2/3 lbs.	750 g
Medium unpeeled tart apples (such as Granny Smith), thinly sliced	2	2
Chopped walnuts	1/2 cup	125 mL
Raisins	1/2 cup	125 mL
CREAMY DILL DRESSING		
Mayonnaise	1/4 cup	60 mL
Sour cream	1/4 cup	60 mL
Olive (or cooking) oil	3 tbsp.	50 mL
Chopped fresh dill	2 tbsp.	30 mL
White wine vinegar	2 tbsp.	30 mL
Granulated sugar	2 tsp.	10 mL
Salt	3/4 tsp.	4 mL
Pepper	1 tsp.	5 mL

Combine first 5 ingredients in large bowl.

Creamy Dill Dressing: Process all 8 ingredients in blender until smooth. Makes about 3/4 cup (175 mL) dressing. Drizzle over salad. Toss. Serves 8.

1 serving: 316 Calories; 18.1 g Total Fat (8.6 g Mono, 6.0 g Poly, 2.5 g Sat); 90 mg Cholesterol; 17 g Carbohydrate; 2 g Fibre; 23 g Protein; 479 mg Sodium

sauerkraut salad

To let the flavours of this delicious German salad mingle, it must be made a day before serving.

Can of wine sauerkraut, rinsed, drained and squeezed dry	28 oz.	796 mL
Chopped celery	1 cup	250 mL
Chopped onion	1 cup	250 mL
Medium green pepper, chopped	1	1
Large peeled tart apple (such as Granny Smith), coarsely grated	1	1
Granulated sugar	3/4 cup	175 mL
Jars of pimiento (2 oz., 57 mL, each), well drained and chopped	2	2

Combine all 7 ingredients in large bowl. Chill for 24 hours to blend flavours. Stir. Store in airtight container in refrigerator for up to 1 week. Makes about 4 cups (1 L).

1/2 cup (125 mL): 124 Calories; 0.3 g Total Fat (trace Mono, 0.1 Poly, 0.1 g Sat); 0 mg Cholesterol; 31 g Carbohydrate; 4 g Fibre; 2 g Protein; 673 mg Sodium

fresh fruit salad

If 'A' is for apple, this arrangement gets an A+ for artful presentation. Try Granny Smith slices with other fruit for new colour and flavour combinations.

Fresh strawberries, halved	6	6
Kiwifruit, cut lengthwise into 6 wedges each	4	4
Seedless red grapes, halved	18	18
Cantaloupe balls or cubes	24	24
Fresh blueberries	1/2 cup	125 mL
Thin unpeeled red apple slices, dipped in lemon juice (see Tip, page 64)	12	12
APRICOT DRESSING		
Dried apricots	8	8
Boiling water, to cover		
Vanilla yogurt	3/4 cup	175 mL

Arrange strawberries in centre of large platter. Arrange next 4 ingredients in circular pattern around strawberries.

Place apple, peel-side up, between fruit on platter.

Apricot Dressing: Put apricots into small bowl. Cover with boiling water. Let stand for about 20 minutes until softened. Drain. Transfer to blender or food processor. Add yogurt. Process until smooth. Makes about 3/4 cup (175 mL) dressing. Drizzle dressing over salad or serve as a dip on the side. Serves 6.

1 serving: 344 Calories; 1.7 g Total Fat (0.4 g Mono, 0.2 g Poly, 0.5 g Sat); 2 mg Cholesterol; 85 g Carbohydrate; 11 g Fibre; 6 g Protein; 40 mg Sodium

apple and cheese grill

Sweet apple slices add crunch to the soft filling. Serve with sliced fresh fruit.

Hard margarine (or butter), softened	6 tbsp.	100 mL
Thick raisin bread slices	8	8
Honey prepared mustard	1/4 cup	60 mL
Deli ham slices (about 6 oz., 170 g)	12	12
Large peeled cooking apple (such as McIntosh), thinly sliced	1	1
Grated sharp Cheddar cheese	1 1/2 cups	375 mL

Spread margarine on bread slices. Place 4 bread slices, margarine-side down, on cutting board. Spread with mustard.

Layer remaining 3 ingredients, in order given, over mustard. Cover with remaining 4 bread slices, margarine-side up. Preheat gas barbecue to medium. Place sandwiches on greased grill. Close lid. Cook for about 6 minutes per side until golden and cheese is melted. Makes 4 sandwiches.

1 sandwich: 612 Calories; 39.4 g Total Fat (19.1 g Mono, 3.1 g Poly, 15.1 g Sat); 71 mg Cholesterol;
43 g Carbohydrate; 3 g Fibre; 23 g Protein; 1345 mg Sodium

creamy veal with apples and rosemary

Apples and cream boil down to a scrumptious sauce for tender veal chops.
Pick up extra rosemary so you can decorate each plate with fresh sprigs.

Cooking oil	1 tbsp.	15 mL
Veal rib (or loin) chops, 3/4 inch	4	4
(2 cm) thick (about 1 lb., 454 g)		
Cooking oil	1 tbsp.	15 mL
Garlic cloves, minced	4	4
Medium peeled tart apples (such as	2	2
Granny Smith), cut into 8 wedges each		
Whipping cream	1 cup	250 mL
Dry (or alcohol-free) red wine	1/4 cup	60 mL
Orange juice	1/4 cup	60 mL
Chopped fresh rosemary	2 tsp.	10 mL
Strip of orange peel (3 inch, 7.5 cm, length)	1	1
Salt	1/2 tsp.	2 mL
Pepper	1/2 tsp.	2 mL

Heat first amount of cooking oil in large frying pan on medium-high. Add veal. Cook for about 3 minutes per side until browned. Remove to large plate.

Heat second amount of cooking oil in same frying pan on medium. Add garlic. Heat and stir for about 30 seconds until fragrant.

Add remaining 8 ingredients. Stir well. Add veal. Simmer, uncovered, for 20 to 25 minutes, turning veal once and stirring mixture several times, until veal is tender and sauce is thickened. Serves 4.

1 serving: 519 Calories; 38.9 g Total Fat (14.4 g Mono, 3.5 g Poly, 18.0 g Sat); 172 mg Cholesterol; 15 g Carbohydrate; 1 g Fibre; 25 g Protein; 427 mg Sodium

apple pork chops

Infused with the sweetness of apples, these pork chops will disappear quickly!

Cooking oil	2 tsp.	10 mL
Bone-in pork chops, trimmed of fat	6	6
Medium peeled cooking apples (such as McIntosh), sliced	3	3
Brown sugar, packed	1/4 cup	60 mL
Ground cinnamon	1/2 tsp.	2 mL

Heat cooking oil in large frying pan on medium-high. Add pork. Cook for about 3 minutes per side until browned. Transfer to ungreased 2 quart (2 L) casserole or small roasting pan.

Arrange apple over pork.

Combine brown sugar and cinnamon in small cup. Sprinkle over apple. Bake, covered, in 350°F (175°C) oven for 60 to 75 minutes until tender. Serves 6.

1 serving: 327 Calories; 11.6 g Total Fat (5.4 g Mono, 1.6 g Poly, 3.6 g Sat); 92 mg Cholesterol; 17 g Carbohydrate; 1 g Fibre; 37 g Protein; 79 mg Sodium

stuffed turkey breast

A fabulous holiday entree without all the leftovers. Or serve this to turkey lovers any time. Use the drippings to make gravy.

SPICED CRAN-APPLE STUFFING

Hard margarine (or butter)	1/4 cup	60 mL
Chopped celery	1/2 cup	125 mL
Chopped onion	1/2 cup	125 mL
Garlic cloves, minced (or 1/2 tsp., 2 mL, powder), optional	2	2
Chopped fresh (or frozen) cranberries	2/3 cup	150 mL
Coarsely grated peeled tart apple (such as Granny Smith)	1/2 cup	125 mL
Fine dry bread crumbs	1/2 cup	125 mL
Brown sugar, packed	1 tbsp.	15 mL
Ground cinnamon	1/4 tsp.	1 mL
Cayenne pepper	1/8 tsp.	0.5 mL
Ground allspice	1/8 tsp.	0.5 mL
Ground nutmeg	1/8 tsp.	0.5 mL
Salt	1/2 tsp.	2 mL
Pepper	1/8 tsp.	0.5 mL
Apple juice (or water), approximately	1 tbsp.	15 mL

TURKEY

Whole bone-in turkey breast	6 lbs.	2.7 kg
Hard margarine (or butter), melted	2 tbsp.	30 mL
Seasoned salt	1/2 tsp.	2 mL
Pepper, sprinkle		

Spiced Cran-Apple Stuffing: Melt margarine in large frying pan on medium-high. Add next 3 ingredients. Cook for about 4 minutes, stirring often, until onion is softened. Remove from heat.

Add next 10 ingredients. Mix well.

Add enough apple juice until stuffing is moist and holds together when squeezed. Makes about 1 1/2 cups (375 mL) stuffing.

Turkey: Cut turkey crosswise into 1 inch (2.5 cm) thick slices right to the bone on both sides. You should be able to cut about 6 slices on each side. Use very sharp knife to keep skin intact. Divide stuffing among "pockets" cut into turkey. Tie butcher's string horizontally around turkey once or twice to hold slices with stuffing together. Place turkey, cut-side up, in medium roasting pan.

Drizzle margarine over turkey. Sprinkle with seasoned salt and pepper. Bake, covered, in 325°F (160°C) oven for 1 3/4 to 2 hours, basting turkey several times with juices from bottom of roasting pan, until meat thermometer inserted into thickest part of breast reads 170°F (77°C). Temperature of stuffing should reach at least 165°F (74°C). Increase heat to 400°F (205°C). Bake, uncovered, for about 15 minutes until skin is browned. Remove butcher's string. Serves 10 to 12.

1 serving: 404 Calories; 13.9 g Total Fat (7.2 g Mono, 2.3 g Poly, 3.3 g Sat); 168 mg Cholesterol; 9 g Carbohydrate; 1 g Fibre; 58 g Protein; 433 mg Sodium

apple-cran squash

This colourful side dish looks gorgeous on a festive table. If you can't find small butternut squash, choose another kind, such as acorn or delicata.

Small butternut squash (about 1 lb., 454 g, each)	2	2
Chopped peeled cooking apple (such as McIntosh)	2 cups	500 mL
Fresh (or frozen, thawed) cranberries	1/3 cup	75 mL
Chopped pecans	1/4 cup	60 mL
Brown sugar, packed	1 1/2 tbsp.	25 mL
Orange juice	1 1/2 tbsp.	25 mL
Butter (or hard margarine), softened	1 tbsp.	15 mL
Ground cinnamon	1/2 tsp.	2 mL
Grated lemon zest	1/4 tsp.	1 mL

Cut squash in half lengthwise. Discard seeds. Arrange squash, cut-side down, on ungreased baking sheet. Bake in 350°F (175°C) oven for 25 minutes.

Combine remaining 8 ingredients in small bowl. Turn squash over, cut-side up. Spoon apple mixture into squash cavities. Bake in 350°F (175°C) oven for about 20 minutes until squash is tender. Serves 4.

1 serving: 214 Calories; 8.5 g Total Fat (5.2 g Mono, 1.7 Poly, 1.1 Sat); 0 mg Cholesterol; 37 g Carbohydrate; 5 g Fibre; 3 g Protein; 45 mg Sodium

apple cabbage

Colourful, delicious and easy to prepare—healthy, too!

Hard margarine (or butter)	2 tbsp.	30 mL
Medium peeled tart apples (such as Granny Smith), thinly sliced	2	2
Shredded green cabbage, lightly packed	2 cups	500 mL
Shredded red cabbage, lightly packed	2 cups	500 mL
Apple juice	1/4 cup	60 mL
Salt	1/4 tsp.	1 mL
Pepper	1/4 tsp.	1 mL

Melt margarine in large frying pan on medium. Add apple. Cook for about 5 minutes, stirring occasionally, until apple starts to soften.

Add remaining 5 ingredients. Heat and stir for about 5 minutes until cabbage is wilted. Do not overcook. Makes about 4 cups (1 L). Serves 6.

1 serving: 77 Calories; 4.1 g Total Fat (2.5 g Mono, 0.5 g Poly, 0.8 g Sat); 0 mg Cholesterol; 11 g Carbohydrate; 2 g Fibre; 1 g Protein; 152 mg Sodium

pepper cabbage relish

When harvest apples spill from the fruit bowl, this makes a marvellous spread!

Chopped peeled tart apple (such as Granny Smith)	3 cups	750 mL
Chopped green pepper	2 cups	500 mL
Chopped red pepper	2 cups	500 mL
Shredded red cabbage	2 cups	500 mL
Chopped hot banana pepper	3/4 cup	175 mL
Coarse (pickling) salt	3 tbsp.	50 mL
Granulated sugar	1 1/2 cups	375 mL
Cornstarch	1 tbsp.	15 mL
Mustard seed	1 tsp.	5 mL
Apple cider vinegar	1 1/2 cups	375 mL

Combine first 6 ingredients in large bowl. Let stand at room temperature for 2 hours. Drain well. Set aside.

Combine next 3 ingredients in large pot or Dutch oven. Add vinegar. Stir. Bring to a boil. Reduce heat to medium-low. Add pepper mixture. Stir. Simmer, uncovered, for about 10 minutes until apple is starting to soften. Fill 5 hot sterile 1/2 pint (250 mL) jars to within 1/2 inch (12 mm) of top. Wipe rims of jars. Place sterile metal lids on jars and screw on metal bands fingertip tight. Do not over-tighten. Process in boiling water bath for 10 minutes (see Note). Remove jars. Cool. Makes about 5 cups (1.5 L).

2 tbsp. (30 mL): 37 Calories; 0.1 g Total Fat (trace Mono, trace Poly, trace Sat); 0 mg Cholesterol; 10 g Carbohydrate; trace Fibre; trace Protein; 447 mg Sodium

Note: Processing time is for elevations 1001 to 3000 feet (306 to 915 m) above sea level. Make adjustment for elevation in your area if necessary.

baked marmalade apples with cinnamon custard

An update of a traditional raisin-stuffed baked apple, this makes a stylish ending to a harvest dinner. Make the custard in advance, then place plastic wrap directly on the surface as it cools. Refrigerate. To heat, place in a heatproof bowl over simmering water and stir until warm.

Butter (or hard margarine), softened	1/4 cup	60 mL
Orange marmalade	3 tbsp.	50 mL
Dried apricots, finely chopped	1/4 cup	60 mL
Pitted dates, finely chopped	1/4 cup	60 mL
Slivered almonds, chopped and toasted (see Tip, page 64)	3 tbsp.	50 mL
Large unpeeled tart apples (such as Granny Smith)	6	6
CINNAMON CUSTARD		
Homogenized milk	2 cups	500 mL
Cinnamon stick (4 inches, 10 cm)	1	1
Egg yolks (large)	4	4
Granulated sugar	1/2 cup	125 mL

Beat butter in medium bowl until smooth and creamy. Add marmalade. Beat well.

Add next 3 ingredients. Stir well.

Carefully remove cores from apples using apple corer, leaving apples whole (photo 1). Cut 1/4 inch (6 mm) off bottom of each core. Press back into base of each apple (photo 2). Score apple skin in several places to prevent skin from shrinking when cooked (photo 3). Fill each apple cavity with 1 1/2 tbsp. (25 mL) butter mixture. Place apples in greased 9 x 13 inch (22 x 33 cm) pan. Bake, uncovered, in 350°F (175°C) oven for about 50 minutes, brushing apples with pan juices 2 or 3 times during baking, until apples are tender.

Cinnamon Custard: Combine milk and cinnamon stick in small saucepan. Heat on medium-high until hot but not boiling. Remove from heat. Let stand for 10 minutes. Remove cinnamon stick.

Beat egg yolks and sugar in small bowl on high until thick and pale. Add 1/4 cup (60 mL) hot milk. Stir well. Slowly add egg yolk mixture to hot milk in saucepan. Cook on medium-low for 15 to 20 minutes, stirring constantly, until boiling and thickened. Makes about 3 cups (750 mL) custard. Serve warm with baked apples. Serves 6.

1 serving: 583 Calories; 25.8 g Total Fat (8.9 g Mono, 2.2 g Poly, 12.3 g Sat); 266 mg Cholesterol; 86 g Carbohydrate; 6 g Fibre; 9 g Protein; 205 mg Sodium

chocolate apple fritters

Sprinkle these tempting morsels with icing sugar just before serving.

All-purpose flour	1 2/3 cups	400 mL
Cocoa, sifted if lumpy	1/3 cup	75 mL
Granulated sugar	3 tbsp.	50 mL
Baking powder	2 tsp.	10 mL
Ground cinnamon	1/2 tsp.	2 mL
Salt	1/4 tsp.	1 mL
Large eggs	3	3
Finely diced peeled cooking apple (such as McIntosh)	2 cups	500 mL
Semi-sweet chocolate chips	1/2 cup	125 mL
Hard margarine (or butter), melted	1 tbsp.	15 mL

Cooking oil, for deep-frying

Icing (confectioner's) sugar, for garnish

Measure first 6 ingredients into large bowl. Stir. Make a well in centre.

Beat eggs in small bowl until frothy. Add next 3 ingredients. Stir. Add to well. Stir until just moistened.

Drop by rounded tablespoonfuls, a few at a time, into hot (375°F, 190°C) cooking oil. When starting to brown, use slotted spoon to turn. When both sides are browned, remove with slotted spoon to paper towels to drain. Cool completely.

Sprinkle with icing sugar. Makes about 35 fritters.

1 fritter: 74 Calories; 4 g Total Fat (2.0 g Mono, 0.8 g Poly, 0.9 g Sat); 18.5 mg Cholesterol; 9 g Carbohydrate; 1 g Fibre; 1 g Protein; 30 mg Sodium

apple strudel

For that Viennese touch, serve with freshly whipped cream or a scoop of vanilla ice cream.

Medium peeled tart apples (such as Granny Smith), sliced	5	5
Brown sugar, packed	3/4 cup	175 mL
Fine dry bread crumbs	1/2 cup	125 mL
Ground cinnamon	1 tsp.	5 mL
Grated orange zest	3/4 tsp.	4 mL
Ground ginger	1/2 tsp.	2 mL
Phyllo pastry sheets, thawed according to package directions	6	6
Butter (or hard margarine), melted	1/3 cup	75 mL
Granulated sugar	1 1/2 tbsp.	25 mL

Combine first 6 ingredients in large bowl.

Lay tea towel on work surface, short end closest to you. Place 1 pastry sheet on towel, lining up short end of sheet with short end of towel. Cover remaining sheets with damp towel to prevent drying. Place second pastry sheet at far end of first sheet with 6 inches (15 cm) overlapping in middle. Working quickly, brush pastry with butter. Layer 2 more pastry sheets on top to make second layer. Brush with butter. Repeat, layering with remaining sheets and butter. Spoon apple mixture onto pastry, 6 inches (15 cm) from closest edge. Fold closest edge of pastry up and over apple mixture. Roll up tightly to enclose apple mixture, using tea towel as guide. Pack any loose apple mixture back into roll on ends. Leave ends open. Place on greased baking sheet. Brush roll with remaining butter.

Sprinkle with granulated sugar. Bake in 350°F (175°C) oven for about 55 minutes until golden and crisp. Let stand for 10 minutes. Cuts into six 2 inch (5 cm) slices.

1 slice: *375 Calories; 12.8 g Total Fat (3.6 g Mono, 1.3 g Poly, 7.1 g Sat); 29 mg Cholesterol; 65 g Carbohydrate; 3 g Fibre; 3 g Protein; 296 mg Sodium*

apple pecan crisps

A saucy fruit dessert with a buttery crumb topping and a sprinkling of pecans.
Add a splash of decadence with a drizzle of cream on top.

Butter (or hard margarine), softened	2 tsp.	10 mL
FILLING		
Large peeled tart apples (such as Granny Smith), chopped	2	2
Water	1/2 cup	125 mL
Raisins	1/4 cup	60 mL
Lemon juice	2 tsp.	10 mL
Brown sugar, packed	1/2 cup	125 mL
Cornstarch	2 tsp.	10 mL
Vanilla extract	1/2 tsp.	2 mL
SHORTBREAD TOPPING		
Crushed shortbread cookies (about 4 cookies)	1/2 cup	125 mL
Ground cinnamon	1/8 tsp.	0.5 mL
Butter (or hard) margarine	2 tbsp.	30 mL
Chopped pecans	1/4 cup	60 mL

Grease four 3/4 cup (175 mL) ramekins with butter.

Filling: Combine first 4 ingredients in medium saucepan. Bring to a boil. Reduce heat to medium-low. Simmer, uncovered, for about 10 minutes, stirring occasionally, until apple is tender.

Combine brown sugar and cornstarch in small bowl. Stir into apple mixture. Heat and stir on medium for about 3 minutes until boiling and slightly thickened. Remove from heat.

Add vanilla. Stir. Divide filling among prepared ramekins.

Shortbread Topping: Combine cookie crumbs and cinnamon in small bowl. Sprinkle over filling.

Melt butter in shallow frying pan on medium. Add pecans. Heat for 3 to 5 minutes, stirring often, until pecans are golden. Sprinkle over crumb mixture. Bake in 350°F (175°C) oven for about 20 minutes until bubbling. Serves 4.

1 serving: 401 Calories; 17.8 g Total Fat (8.1 g Mono, 2.3 g Poly, 6.5 g Sat); 25 mg Cholesterol; 62 g Carbohydrate; 2 g Fibre; 2 g Protein; 178 mg Sodium

applesauce rice pudding

Use up leftover rice—a terrific dessert ready in less than 25 minutes!

Granulated sugar	1/2 cup	125 mL
Cornstarch	2 tbsp.	30 mL
Can of evaporated milk	13 1/2 oz.	385 mL
Milk	1/2 cup	125 mL
Applesauce	2/3 cup	150 mL
Cooked short grain white rice (not instant), about 7/8 cup (200 mL) uncooked	1 1/2 cups	375 mL
Raisins	1/2 cup	125 mL
Ground cinnamon	1/2 tsp.	2 mL
Large egg	1	1
Milk	1/4 cup	60 mL
Vanilla extract	1 1/4 tsp.	6 mL

Ground cinnamon, sprinkle

Combine sugar and cornstarch in medium saucepan. Stir in evaporated milk and first amount of milk.

Add applesauce. Stir well.

Add next 3 ingredients. Stir. Bring to a boil on medium, stirring occasionally. Reduce heat to medium-low. Simmer, uncovered, for 5 minutes, stirring occasionally.

Beat egg and second amount of milk in small bowl until frothy. Stir into rice mixture. Heat and stir for about 5 minutes until boiling and thickened.

Add vanilla. Stir.

Sprinkle individual servings with cinnamon. Makes about 4 2/3 cups (1.15 L). Serves 6.

1 serving: 322 Calories; 6.7 g Total Fat (2.1 g Mono, 0.4 g Poly, 3.8 g Sat); 57 mg Cholesterol; 57 g Carbohydrate; 1 g Fibre; 9 g Protein; 102 mg Sodium

apple croissant pudding

This brandy-flavoured pudding makes good use of day-old croissants.

Chopped dried apple	2/3 cup	150 mL
Medium croissants	4	4
Apple jelly	1/3 cup	75 mL
Large eggs	4	4
Milk	2 cups	500 mL
Whipping cream	2 cups	500 mL
Granulated sugar	2/3 cup	150 mL
Brandy (or 2 tsp., 10 mL, brandy extract)	3 tbsp.	50 mL

Ground cinnamon, sprinkle

Icing (confectioner's) sugar, for garnish

Place apple in greased 2 quart (2 L) shallow baking dish.

Cut croissants in half horizontally. Spread jelly on cut sides. Cut each half into 3 equal pieces. Arrange, jelly-side up and slightly overlapping, over apple.

Whisk next 5 ingredients in large bowl or 8 cup (2 L) liquid measure until smooth. Carefully pour half over croissants. Let stand for 10 minutes. Stir remaining cream mixture. Carefully pour over croissants.

Sprinkle with cinnamon. Place baking dish in larger baking pan. Slowly pour boiling water into baking pan until water comes halfway up sides of baking dish. Bake, uncovered, in 325°F (160°C) oven for 1 1/2 to 1 3/4 hours until set and knife inserted in centre comes out clean. Remove dish from pan. Let stand for 20 minutes before serving.

Sprinkle with icing sugar. Serves 8.

1 serving: 490 Calories; 28.7 g Total Fat (8.5 g Mono, 1.3 g Poly, 16.8 g Sat); 202 mg Cholesterol; 49 g Carbohydrate; 2 g Fibre; 9 g Protein; 286 mg Sodium

glazed apple tart

Rings of tart apple slices brushed with a sweet apple glaze celebrate the bounty of this delicious fruit. Bake an extra one to wrap well in plastic and freeze. Defrost and heat at 300°F (150°C) for 30 minutes for that fresh harvest flavour.

Pastry for 9 inch
(22 cm) pie shell

Butter (or hard margarine), softened	1/4 cup	60 mL
Granulated sugar	1/3 cup	75 mL
Large egg	1	1
Almond extract	1/2 tsp.	2 mL
Ground almonds	2/3 cup	150 mL
All-purpose flour	3 tbsp.	50 mL
Seedless raspberry jam (not jelly)	1/4 cup	60 mL
Thinly sliced peeled tart apple (such as Granny Smith)	3 cups	750 mL
Granulated sugar	2 tbsp.	30 mL

GLAZE
Apple jelly	1/2 cup	125 mL

Roll out pastry on lightly floured surface to fit ungreased 9 inch (22 cm) tart pan with fluted sides and removable bottom. Carefully lift pastry and press into bottom and up side of pan. Trim edge. Place pan on ungreased baking sheet (see Tip, page 64).

Cream butter and first amount of sugar in medium bowl. Add egg and extract. Beat well.

Add almonds and flour. Stir until mixture resembles fine paste.

Spread jam evenly on bottom of pastry shell. Spread almond mixture on top of jam.

Combine apple and second amount of sugar in medium bowl. Toss. Arrange apple, slightly overlapping in fan pattern, on top of almond mixture to cover. Bake on bottom rack in 375°F (190°C) oven for about 1 1/4 hours until pastry is golden and apple just starts to brown.

Glaze: Microwave apple jelly, uncovered, in small microwave-safe bowl on medium (50%) until melted. Brush over hot tart. Let stand in pan on wire rack to cool. Cuts into 8 wedges.

1 wedge: 370 Calories; 18 g Total Fat (7.6 g Mono, 3.3 g Poly, 6.1 g Sat); 39 mg Cholesterol; 50 g Carbohydrate; 2 g Fibre; 4 g Protein; 171 mg Sodium

caramel apple pie

A tart apple pie with a beautifully glazed lattice top.

Pastry for 2 crust 9 inch (22 cm) pie

Large egg	1	1
Block of cream cheese, softened	8 oz.	250 g
Caramel ice cream topping	3/4 cup	175 mL
Lemon juice	1 tbsp.	15 mL
Ground cinnamon	1/2 tsp.	2 mL
Medium peeled tart apples (such as Granny Smith), thinly sliced	5	5
Pecan halves, toasted (see Tip, page 64) and finely chopped	1 1/2 cups	375 mL
Brown sugar, packed	1/4 cup	60 mL
Egg yolk (large), fork-beaten	1	1

Divide pastry into 2 portions, making 1 portion slightly larger than the other. Shape each portion into slightly flattened disc. Roll out larger portion on lightly floured surface to about 1/8 inch (3 mm) thickness. Line 9 inch (22 cm) pie plate. Trim, leaving 1/2 inch (12 mm) overhang.

Beat next 5 ingredients in large bowl until smooth.

Add apple. Stir until coated. Sprinkle bottom of pie shell with pecans. Spoon apple mixture into pie shell. Spread evenly. Sprinkle with brown sugar. Roll out smaller portion of pastry on lightly floured surface to 9 x 11 inch (22 x 28 cm) rectangle. Cut into eleven 3/4 inch (2 cm) strips with fluted pastry cutter. Dampen edge of shell and both ends of pastry strips with water. Place 6 strips, side-by-side, equally spaced apart, on top of filling. Repeat with remaining strips in opposite direction. Trim strips at crust edge, leaving 1 inch (2.5 cm) overhang. Moisten and tuck ends under crust. Crimp decorative edge to seal.

Brush pastry with egg yolk. Bake on bottom rack in 450°F (230°C) oven for 10 minutes. Reduce heat to 350°F (175°C). Bake for 45 to 50 minutes until apple is tender and crust is golden. Serve warm. Cuts into 8 wedges.

1 wedge: 599 Calories; 38.5 g Total Fat (18.3 g Mono, 5.8 g Poly, 11.9 g Sat); 88 mg Cholesterol; 62 g Carbohydrate; 3 g Fibre; 7 g Protein; 422 mg Sodium

apple pumpkin pie

You can cut this recipe in half to make just one pie, but experience has shown us that everyone will ask for seconds!

Pastry for two 9 inch (22 cm) pie shells

Brown sugar, packed	1/2 cup	125 mL
Vanilla custard powder	1/4 cup	60 mL
Chopped peeled cooking apple (such as McIntosh)	4 cups	1 L
Brown sugar, packed	2/3 cup	150 mL
Ground cinnamon	1 tsp.	5 mL
Ground ginger	1 tsp.	5 mL
Ground allspice	1/2 tsp.	2 mL
Ground nutmeg	1/2 tsp.	2 mL
Salt	1/2 tsp.	2 mL
Large eggs	4	4
Can of pure pumpkin (no spices)	14 oz.	398 mL
Can of skim evaporated milk	13 1/2 oz.	385 mL

Milk (optional)

Divide pastry into 2 equal portions. Shape portions into slightly flattened discs. Roll out 1 portion at a time on lightly floured surface to about 1/8 inch (3 mm) thickness. Line two 9 inch (22 cm) pie plates. Trim, leaving 1/2 inch (12 mm) overhang. Roll under and crimp decorative edges, or use scraps of dough to create decorative edges, such as leaf cut-outs.

Measure first amount of brown sugar and custard powder into large bowl. Stir. Add apple. Mix well. Divide between pie shells. Spread evenly.

Measure next 6 ingredients into same bowl. Stir.

Beat in next 3 ingredients until smooth. Spoon over apple mixture. Set any cut-outs on top of pastry edge.

Brush pastry edge with milk. Bake on bottom rack in 375°F (190°C) oven for about 45 minutes until knife inserted in centre comes out moist but clean. Makes 2 pies, each cutting into 8 wedges, for a total of 16 wedges.

1 wedge: 307 Calories; 12.1 g Total Fat (3.1 g Mono, 0.9 g Poly, 2.2 g Sat); 66 mg Cholesterol; 45 g Carbohydrate; 1 g Fibre; 6 g Protein; 357 mg Sodium

dutch apple cream pie

Apple slices suspended in a custard-like sauce—does it get any better than this?

Pastry for 9 inch (22 cm) pie shell

Granulated sugar	1/2 cup	125 mL
All-purpose flour	3 tbsp.	50 mL
Cornstarch	2 tbsp.	30 mL
Sliced peeled cooking apples (such as McIntosh)	6 cups	1.5 L
Large egg, fork-beaten	1	1
Sour cream	1 cup	250 mL
Granulated sugar	1/4 cup	60 mL
Ground cinnamon	1/2 tsp.	2 mL

Roll out pastry on lightly floured surface to about 1/8 inch (3 mm) thickness. Line 9 inch (22 cm) pie plate. Trim, leaving 1/2 inch (12 mm) overhang. Roll under and crimp decorative edge.

Combine next 3 ingredients in large bowl. Add apple. Stir until coated. Spoon into pie shell. Spread evenly.

Mix egg and sour cream in small bowl. Pour over apple mixture.

Combine second amount of sugar and cinnamon in small dish. Sprinkle over sour cream mixture. Bake on bottom rack in 350°F (175°C) oven for about 1 1/4 hours until crust is golden and apple is tender-crisp. Cool to room temperature before cutting. Cuts into 8 wedges.

1 wedge: 282 Calories; 10.4 g Total Fat (4.0 g Mono, 1.0 g Poly, 4.6 g Sat); 39 mg Cholesterol; 46 g Carbohydrate; 2 g Fibre; 3 g Protein; 124 mg Sodium

apple loaf

Freeze this in slices for fast breakfasts on busy mornings.

All-purpose flour	2 cups	500 mL
Chopped walnuts, toasted (see Tip, page 64)	1/2 cup	125 mL
Baking powder	1 tsp.	5 mL
Baking soda	1/2 tsp.	2 mL
Salt	1/2 tsp.	2 mL
Hard margarine (or butter), softened	1/2 cup	125 mL
Granulated sugar	1 cup	250 mL
Large eggs	2	2
Milk	1/3 cup	75 mL
Vanilla extract	1 tsp.	5 mL
Coarsely grated unpeeled tart apple (such as Granny Smith)	1 cup	250 mL

Measure first 5 ingredients into large bowl. Stir. Make a well in centre. Set aside.

Cream margarine and sugar in medium bowl. Add eggs 1 at a time, beating well after each addition. Add milk and vanilla. Beat well.

Add apple. Stir. Add to well in flour mixture. Stir until just moistened. Spread in greased 9 x 5 x 3 inch (22 x 12.5 x 7.5 cm) loaf pan. Bake in 350°F (175°C) oven for about 1 hour until wooden pick inserted in centre comes out clean. Let stand in pan for 10 minutes. Remove loaf from pan and place on wire rack to cool. Cuts into 16 slices.

1 slice: 207 Calories; 9.2 g Total Fat (4.7 g Mono, 2.3 g Poly, 1.7 g Sat); 27 mg Cholesterol; 28 g Carbohydrate; 1 g Fibre; 4 g Protein; 219 mg Sodium

apple streusel muffins

A fresh muffin and a cup of something hot—now that's comfort food!

All-purpose flour	1 1/2 cups	375 mL
Granulated sugar	1/2 cup	125 mL
Baking powder	1 tbsp.	15 mL
Salt	1/2 tsp.	2 mL
Large egg	1	1
Milk	2/3 cup	150 mL
Cooking oil	1/4 cup	60 mL
Coarsely grated peeled cooking apple (such as McIntosh)	3/4 cup	175 mL
TOPPING		
Brown sugar, packed	1/4 cup	60 mL
All-purpose flour	2 tbsp.	30 mL
Ground cinnamon	1/8 tsp.	0.5 mL
Cold hard margarine (or butter)	1 tbsp.	15 mL

Measure first 4 ingredients into large bowl. Stir. Make a well in centre.

Combine next 3 ingredients in small bowl. Add apple. Stir. Add to well. Stir until just moistened. Fill 12 greased muffin cups 3/4 full.

Topping: Combine first 3 ingredients in small bowl. Cut in margarine until mixture resembles coarse crumbs. Sprinkle on batter. Bake in 400ºF (205ºC) oven for 15 to 20 minutes until wooden pick inserted in centre of muffin comes out clean. Let stand in pan for 5 minutes. Remove muffins from pan and place on wire rack to cool. Makes 12 muffins.

1 muffin: 196 Calories; 6.6 g Total Fat (3.7 g Mono, 1.7 g Poly, 0.4 g Sat); 19 mg Cholesterol; 29 g Carbohydrate; 1 g Fibre; 3 g Protein; 218 mg Sodium

apple almond cake

Put this together on a chilly evening and watch how the scent of apples and toasted almonds draws everyone into the kitchen.

Butter (or hard margarine), softened	1/2 cup	125 mL
Granulated sugar	2/3 cup	150 mL
Large eggs	2	2
All-purpose flour	1 1/2 cups	375 mL
Baking powder	2 tsp.	10 mL
Ground cinnamon	1 tsp.	5 mL
Salt	1/4 tsp.	1 mL
Buttermilk (see Tip, page 64)	1/2 cup	125 mL
Large peeled tart apple (such as Granny Smith), coarsely grated	1	1
Sliced almonds, toasted (see Tip, page 64)	1/3 cup	75 mL

Cream butter and sugar in medium bowl. Add eggs 1 at a time, beating well after each addition.

Combine next 4 ingredients in small bowl.

Add flour mixture to butter mixture in 3 additions, alternating with buttermilk in 2 additions, stirring after each addition until just combined. Line bottom of greased 8 inch (20 cm) springform pan with waxed paper. Pour batter into pan. Spread evenly.

Combine apple and almonds in separate small bowl. Spoon evenly over batter. Bake in 350°F (175°C) oven for about 1 hour until wooden pick inserted in centre comes out clean. Let stand in pan on wire rack for 10 minutes. Run knife around inside edge of pan to loosen cake. Let stand in pan on wire rack until completely cooled. Remove to serving plate, discarding waxed paper from bottom of cake. Cuts into 8 wedges.

1 wedge: 330 Calories; 16.3 g Total Fat (5.6 g Mono, 1.3 g Poly, 8.3 g Sat); 87 mg Cholesterol; 42 g Carbohydrate; 2 g Fibre; 6 g Protein; 325 mg Sodium

apple spice cake

With its praline topping, this dessert takes the cake! Bake extra without the topping to freeze. Spread praline mixture over thawed cake and broil.

Hard margarine (or butter), softened	1/2 cup	125 mL
Granulated sugar	1 1/4 cups	300 mL
Large eggs	2	2
Can of applesauce	14 oz.	398 mL
All-purpose flour	2 1/2 cups	625 mL
Baking soda	1 1/2 tsp.	7 mL
Ground cinnamon	1 1/2 tsp.	7 mL
Ground cloves	1/2 tsp.	2 mL
Salt	1/2 tsp.	2 mL
Baking powder	1/4 tsp.	1 mL
Raisins	1 cup	250 mL
PRALINE TOPPING		
Hard margarine (or butter)	6 tbsp.	100 mL
Brown sugar, packed	2/3 cup	150 mL
Milk	2 tbsp.	30 mL
Chopped pecans	1/2 cup	125 mL
Medium coconut	1/2 cup	125 mL

Cream margarine and sugar in large bowl. Add eggs 1 at a time, beating well after each addition. Add applesauce. Beat well.

Combine next 6 ingredients in small bowl. Add to applesauce mixture. Beat well.

Stir in raisins until well distributed. Pour into greased 9 x 13 inch (22 x 33 cm) pan. Spread evenly. Bake in 350°F (175°C) oven for 30 to 35 minutes until wooden pick inserted in centre comes out clean.

Praline Topping: Combine all 5 ingredients in small saucepan. Heat and stir on medium until brown sugar is dissolved. Spread over cake. Broil on top rack in oven for 3 to 5 minutes until bubbly. Cuts into 16 pieces.

1 piece: 357 Calories; 15.1 g Total Fat (8.2 g Mono, 1.8 g Poly, 4.1 g Sat); 27 mg Cholesterol; 54 g Carbohydrate; 2 g Fibre; 4 g Protein 341 mg Sodium

apple cake

This cinnamon-scented cake with its delicious topping travels easily to any happy gathering.

Large egg	1	1
Granulated sugar	1/2 cup	125 mL
Milk	1/2 cup	125 mL
Cooking oil	1/4 cup	60 mL
All-purpose flour	1 1/2 cups	375 mL
Baking powder	1 tbsp.	15 mL
Ground cinnamon	1/2 tsp.	2 mL
Salt	1/2 tsp.	2 mL
Chopped peeled cooking apple (such as McIntosh)	1 1/2 cups	375 mL
TOPPING		
Brown sugar, packed	1/3 cup	75 mL
All-purpose flour	2 tbsp.	30 mL
Hard margarine (or butter), melted	1 1/2 tbsp.	25 mL
Ground cinnamon	1/2 tsp.	2 mL

Beat first 4 ingredients with whisk in large bowl.

Combine next 4 ingredients in small bowl. Add to egg mixture. Stir well.

Add apple. Stir until well distributed. Pour into greased 8 x 8 inch (20 x 20 cm) pan. Spread evenly.

Topping: Combine all 4 ingredients in small bowl. Stir until mixture resembles coarse crumbs. Sprinkle over batter. Bake in 400°F (205°C) oven for about 30 minutes until wooden pick inserted in centre comes out clean. Cuts into 9 pieces.

1 piece: 267 Calories; 9.6 g Total Fat (5.5 g Mono, 2.3 g Poly, 1.2 g Sat); 25 mg Cholesterol; 42 g Carbohydrate; 1 g Fibre; 4 g Protein; 299 mg Sodium

brown betty

If your neighbours show up with a bushel of apples, reward them with a generous helping of this dessert. You can try other fruit with this recipe. Omit the apple and use sliced peaches or apricots. Rhubarb needs an extra 1/2 cup (125 mL) sugar. Bake as directed.

Sliced peeled cooking apples (such as McIntosh)	6 cups	1.5 L
Granulated sugar	3/4 cup	175 mL
TOPPING		
All-purpose flour	1 1/4 cups	300 mL
Brown sugar, packed	3/4 cup	175 mL
Salt	1/2 tsp.	2 mL
Cold hard margarine (or butter), cut up	1/2 cup	125 mL

Place apple in ungreased 3 quart (3 L) shallow baking dish. Sprinkle with sugar.

Topping: Combine first 3 ingredients in medium bowl. Cut in margarine until mixture resembles coarse crumbs. Sprinkle evenly over apple. Press down lightly. Bake, uncovered, in 375°F (190°C) oven for about 40 minutes until apple is tender. Serves 8.

1 serving: 392 Calories; 12.5 g Total Fat (7.9 g Mono, 1.4 g Poly, 2.6 g Sat); 0 mg Cholesterol; 70 g Carbohydrate; 2 g Fibre; 2 g Protein; 299 mg Sodium

apple rhubarb crumble

In a hurry? Don't bother peeling the apples. Just wash well, slice and toss into the saucepan.

Large peeled tart apples (such as Granny Smith), cut into eight wedges each	4	4
Granulated sugar	1/4 cup	60 mL
Water	1/4 cup	60 mL
Chopped fresh (or frozen, thawed) rhubarb	2 cups	500 mL
CRUMBLE TOPPING		
All-purpose flour	1 cup	250 mL
Brown sugar, packed	2/3 cup	150 mL
Baking powder	2 tsp.	10 mL
Ground cinnamon	1/2 tsp.	2 mL
Ground cloves	1/4 tsp.	1 mL
Cold hard margarine (or butter), cut up	1/2 cup	125 mL

Combine first 3 ingredients in large saucepan. Cook, covered, on low for about 10 minutes until apple is just tender. Drain.

Add rhubarb. Stir. Spoon into greased 1 1/2 quart (1.5 L) casserole.

Crumble Topping: Combine first 5 ingredients in medium bowl. Cut in margarine until mixture resembles coarse crumbs. Sprinkle over apple mixture. Bake, uncovered, in 350°F (175°C) oven for about 30 minutes until top is browned. Serves 6.

1 serving: 382 Calories; 16.6 g Total Fat (10.5 g Mono, 1.8 g Poly, 3.4 g Sat); 0 mg Cholesterol; 58 g Carbohydrate; 3 g Fibre; 3 g Protein; 324 mg Sodium

recite index

topical tips

Apples aid ripening: Because apples produce a gas called ethylene, they can be placed in a bag of unripened fruit to quicken the ripening process.

Fresh apple pieces: To keep apple slices or cubes from turning brown, dip them in lemon juice.

Tart pan safety: Placing the tart pan on a baking sheet provides a safe way to remove the hot pan from the oven.

Toasting nuts, seeds or coconut: Cooking times will vary for each type of nut—so never toast them together. For small amounts, place ingredient in an ungreased shallow frying pan. Heat on medium for 3 to 5 minutes, stirring often, until golden. For larger amounts, spread ingredient evenly in an ungreased shallow pan. Bake in 350°F (175°C) oven for 5 to 10 minutes, stirring or shaking often, until golden.

Making soured milk: To make soured milk, measure 1 tbsp. (15 mL) white vinegar or lemon juice into a 1 cup (250 mL) liquid measure. Add enough milk to make 1 cup (250 mL). Stir. Let stand for 1 minute.

Nutrition Information Guidelines

Each recipe is analyzed using the Canadian Nutrient File from Health Canada, which is based on the United States Department of Agriculture (USDA) Nutrient Database.

- If more than one ingredient is listed (such as "butter or hard margarine"), or if a range is given (1 – 2 tsp., 5 – 10 mL), only the first ingredient or first amount is analyzed.

- For meat, poultry and fish, the serving size per person is based on the recommended 4 oz. (113 g) uncooked weight (without bone), which is 2 – 3 oz. (57 – 85 g) cooked weight (without bone)— approximately the size of a deck of playing cards.

- Milk used is 1% M.F. (milk fat), unless otherwise stated.

- Cooking oil used is canola oil, unless otherwise stated.

- Ingredients indicating "sprinkle," "optional," or "for garnish" are not included in the nutrition information.

- The fat in recipes and combination foods can vary greatly depending on the sources and types of fats used in each specific ingredient. For these reasons, the count of saturated, monounsaturated and polyunsaturated fats may not add up to the total fat content.